COURAGE CALLS TO COURAGE EVERYWHERE

Also by Jeanette Winterson

FICTION
Oranges Are Not the Only Fruit
Boating for Beginners
The Passion
Sexing the Cherry
Written on the Body
Art & Lies
Gut Symmetries
The World and Other Places (short stories)
The PowerBook
Lighthousekeeping
Weight
The Stone Gods
Midsummer Nights (ed)
(short stories inspired by the opera)
The Daylight Gate
The Gap of Time
Christmas Days
(short stories and recipes for Xmas)

NON-FICTION
Art Objects (essays)
Why Be Happy When You Could Be Normal? (memoir)
Land (with Antony Gormley)

FOR CHILDREN
The Lion, The Unicorn and Me
The King of Capri
Tanglewreck
The Battle of the Sun

COURAGE CALLS TO COURAGE EVERYWHERE is a timely and inspiring call to arms by one of Britain's most acclaimed and important writers. Whilst recognising how far women have come in the hundred years since getting the vote, Jeanette Winterson also insists that we must all do much more if we are to achieve true equality.

Examining recent women's rights movements, the worlds of politics, technology and social media, and changes in the law, Winterson calls out all the ways in which women still face discrimination and disadvantage. Like the women who won the right to vote, we need to shout loud, reach out, be courageous and finish the job.

Also included in this volume is Emmeline Pankhurst's landmark Suffragette speech, 'Freedom or Death', which she delivered in 1913.

COURAGE CALLS TO COURAGE EVERYWHERE

JEANETTE WINTERSON

CANONGATE

First published in Great Britain in 2018 by Canongate Books Ltd,
14 High Street, Edinburgh EH1 1TE

canongate.co.uk

1

Courage Calls to Courage Everywhere was originally conceived
as a speech, delivered by Jeanette Winterson as the 2018
Richard Dimbleby Lecture on 7 July 2018 and broadcast on BBC One

British Library Cataloguing-in-Publication Data
A catalogue record for this book is available on
request from the British Library

ISBN 978 1 78689 621 6

Typeset in Centaur MT by Palimpsest Book Production Ltd,
Falkirk, Stirlingshire

Printed and bound in Great Britain by
Clays Ltd, Elcograf S.p.A.

To Susie Orbach – who knows that women must keep re-inventing the wheel.

Courage Calls to
Courage Everywhere

In 1908 the Women's Social and Political Union marketed a board game called Suffragetto.

Twenty-one green pieces – the militant suffragettes – had to break through police lines and enter the House of Commons. The twenty-one black pieces were the manly constables paid to stop them. As a twist, the burly black police pieces had to be prevented by the girls in green from storming the Albert Hall and breaking up a Suffragette rally.

Who says feminists don't have a sense of humour?

In 1908, in the UK, women seemed as far away as ever from winning the right to vote. Ten years later, victory was theirs.

If the Suffragettes could time-travel, and be with us now, they would be astonished at how much has changed for women in just one hundred years.

Women are lawyers, doctors, scientists, journalists, artists, economists and entrepreneurs.

The police pieces in our board game of Suffragetto were all male because women couldn't join the force a hundred years ago. Now, in 2018, Cressida Dick has the top job as the first female Commissioner of the Metropolitan Police.

A hundred years ago there were no women MPs. Now there are 208. And whatever your politics, wince or cheer, the UK is counting its second female Prime Minister.

In Scotland, Nicola Sturgeon is First Minister.

When I was writing this essay as a lecture

for TV, I was thinking of calling it *Women's Equality: The Horrible History* – but 'history' implies the past, and suggests that the work is done, at least in the Western world.

But a woman's work is never done. So before we look at some of the challenges women still face, and before we risk a little futurology, let's time-travel back to 1918; the first Representation of the People Act to include women.

The Act gave the vote to all men over twenty-one, and to some women aged thirty and above.

The reason for the age discrepancy?

So many men had been slaughtered during the First World War that to enfranchise women on the same terms as men would have given women the numerical majority. That was too frightening to contemplate – so women had to wait another ten years, until 1928, for full equality at the ballot box.

Even then, the *Daily Mail* called it 'The Flapper Vote' and questioned the sanity of giving 'girls of twenty-one' a say in the running of the State. But those girls of twenty-one were often women who had been working full-time since they were fourteen years old.

Votes for Women wasn't only a middle-class movement, any more than the campaign #MeToo is a yacht-load of celebrities. Then, as now, women from all walks of life came together to fight injustice and inequality, at home, in the workplace, at the ballot box.

The bravest were the poorest; in London, activists included working women from the factories that made matches or tinned food. And across the country, on their half-day off, servants who could lose their jobs if found out crowded into the Suffragette rallies.

In Lancashire, cotton workers slogging twelve hours a day in the mills rallied to the Pankhursts' northern powerhouse that started in Manchester: the Women's Social and Political Union.

Manchester has never been a sit-down-and-shut-up kind of city. It was the birthplace of the Industrial Revolution – home of the Trades Union Movement. Marx and Engels walking the blackened, deafening streets, and asking if human beings who were clever enough to invent the vast machinery of industrialisation couldn't invent a fairer, more equitable distribution of wealth?

And what about a fairer, more equitable distribution of power?

Working men had few enough rights, but they were, in law, persons in their own right. Women were not. Women, legally, were grouped with children and the insane.

Votes for Women was as much about changing the law in regard to the status of women as it was about equality at the ballot box.

In Manchester, working women, more used to the rough and tumble of life than their middle-class sisters, weren't afraid of the Pankhursts' call to go militant.

I was born in Manchester and a hundred years ago I'd have been clattering in my clogs down to the mill – so I love the story of mill-girl Annie Kenney. She isn't too well known but she's a heroine of mine.

Annie had started half-time in the cotton factory at ten years old – going full-time at thirteen. She'd lost a finger in the looms. She paid her way and she paid her taxes. Annie wanted the vote.

In 1905 at the Free Trade Hall in Manchester, Annie turned up to a political meeting held by the Liberals. The Suffragettes had written to the Liberals asking to send a deputation that day, but they were ignored.

Sir Edward Grey – later the Foreign Secretary, Lord Grey, who would lead Britain into the First World War – was speaking when Annie Kenney stood on her chair and shouted: *'Will the Liberal Government give the vote to women?'*

Annie was tiny – but she knew how to yell. You try talking quietly above the racket of a hundred looms.

Annie was ignored so she yelled again – louder.

This time men dragged her off her chair, but Christabel Pankhurst, who was sitting nearby, unfurled a banner that said 'Votes For Women!'

Plain-clothes policemen came to force both women to leave. They were dragged down the aisles, men jeering either side. Annie shouted back: *'If I am forced to leave this hall I shall hold a meeting outside!'*

Actually – as she was from Oldham – she said: *'If ah'm forced t'leev this 'all ah shall 'old a meetin' ahtside!'*

Both women were arrested. Christabel Pankhurst got a week in jail and Annie Kenney got three days.

Jail? For interrupting a meeting?

Clearly, men don't like being interrupted.

Women, though, had had enough of being ignored or double-crossed by men in power.

It's often forgotten that the campaign for women's suffrage started back in 1867. Women are patient – and these women were law-abiding and God-fearing – but, to quote my mother, the late Mrs Winterson: 'The Bible tells us to turn the other cheek but there are only so many cheeks in a day.'

From that day forward, women went militant. Middle-class women, aristocratic women, working women. Women confronted politicians at meetings, at their homes, even on the golf course.

Women chained themselves to railings. Women blew up letterboxes – the Victorians and Edwardians loved writing letters, and the Empire depended on paperwork – so getting the post blown up was *really* annoying.

Women smashed windows, hiding hammers in their muffs – and as muffs had sexual connotations, men began to worry about what was coming next.

Women lobbed slates off the roofs of meeting houses where MPs had refused to take a question on Votes for Women – and I want you to think of those women, climbing up in their full skirts, perched on the roof ridge with their axes, probably in their muffs . . .

On one occasion police turned fire hoses full-blast on a pair of slate-smashers because the firemen refused to do it. The women had to spend the night in their cells in soaking clothes.

Women who went to prison and who went on hunger strike were force-fed in the most brutal way, using thick rubber tubes that caused permanent injury to their throats and digestive systems.

Women who went on marches used cardboard to pad their ribs to prevent them from being broken by male yobs, or police truncheons.

Who was doing the violence here? The women? Or the men?

There's still some debate around women's militancy: did it do the cause any good?

Winston Churchill claimed the militants could never have won the vote. Conventional readings of the suffrage movement opine that only when women had 'proved' themselves in the First World War could sufficient support be mobilised in government, and in the country, to recognise women – well, some of them – as full citizens.

Votes for Women fired no shots. Britain sent more than six million men into the First World War. Force, it seems, only becomes violence when it threatens the status quo.

Unreasonably, but unsurprisingly, one of the major arguments put forward by opponents of Votes for Women was that women weren't called upon to defend country and empire – in other words, to fight. But when women showed that they were more than capable of putting up a fight, their newfound unwomanliness became yet another reason why women must not be allowed the vote.

But there were so many reasons.

Here's an extract from a 1913 bestseller by medical doctor Sir Almroth Wright called *The Unexpurgated Case Against Women's Suffrage*:

No doctor can ever lose sight of the fact that the mind of woman is always threatened with danger from the reverberations of her physiological emergencies . . . It is with such thoughts that the doctor lets his eyes rest on the militant suffragist. He cannot shut them to the fact that there is mixed up with the women's movement much mental disorder . . .

Mad women, unstable women, violent women . . .

———

After the *Titanic* went down in 1912, the British press urgently needed to turn a national fiasco into a story of national heroism. They realised this could be done by having a crack at the crazy women blowing up letterboxes. The famous self-sacrifice of the rule of the sea – to rescue women and children first – morphed into the catchy headline: *BOATS OR VOTES.*

So women wanted equality with men? asked the papers. Would those same women be happy to go down with the ship instead of being chivalrously lowered into the too-few lifeboats? This tedious bit of triumphalism became a great drawing-room favourite. If they'd had printed T-shirts back then, you can be sure BOATS OR VOTES would have been the latest Edwardian must-have.*

Of course, nobody asked whether putting

---

* Along with a Husky maybe, as the cheating Norwegian feminist Amundsen had just beaten our hero, Scott, to the South Pole. By the way, one year later, in 1913 Norway would give women the vote.

women in charge of health and safety at big companies like the White Star Line might have resulted in the *Titanic* carrying enough lifeboats to start with – instead of some important bloke deciding that lifeboats spoilt the view and were a waste of space.

But women were not going to get important jobs in industry because a woman's place was in the home – except for the millions of working-class women whose place was also in the factory, or in shop-work, or skivvying in someone else's home.

The reasons why women can't, don't, shouldn't or couldn't, were legion – and they still are.

Even now, while the row rages over women in the boardroom or in the top jobs, men still say – and they believe it – that women don't want the pressure, or they don't have the experience, or that they couldn't manage the hours alongside a family – because although we're told a child needs a father as well as a mother, the father isn't expected to actually look after his children. Some fathers do take equal parental responsibility, and fathers, mothers and children are better for it. The problem is that as long as society sees parenting as optional for men and obligatory for women, we'll be stuck with gender inequality based not on capacity – what a woman *can* do – but on sex discrimination – what she *can't* do.

Sex differences are biological. Gender differences are social constructs.

———————

The belief that men and women have different brains, brains that are hard-wired differently – why girls like dolls (don't mention Action Man), why boys are better at science (actually they're not) – is nothing more than old-fashioned gendered essentialism. Show me two brains in two buckets and tell me which one is female. The adult human brain weighs around 3lb and although it looks like a cauliflower, it is best described as a computer made of meat. How we programme it is up to us.

Let me give you an example from the good old days of Votes for Women about how we (I mean men, don't I?) have tried to sex the brain.

'Anorexia Scholastica'.

When women were campaigning for the vote, they were also campaigning for education for women. Around the turn of the century education for women of any class was not a priority. Posh women got a tutor. Other women would be lucky to read and write and add up. As women started to question their condition of forced ignorance doctors invented a special and splendid physiological disorder just for girls. Boys were not affected. 'Anorexia scholastica' manifested as debilitating thinness resulting from too much mental stimulus. Mathematics was thought to be a particular problem for women, diverting energy from the reproductive system.

This is nearly as mad as 5,000 years earlier, when the Greeks came up with the wandering womb to explain why women could not be citizens. The Greek word for uterus is *hystera*. Women are hysterical – unfit for anything but our biological purpose, because our uterus wanders about.

But while we are laughing at the past, I have to remind you that the American Psychiatric Association didn't drop hysteria as a mental disorder affecting women until 1952. Women put into mental institutions because they suffered from hysteria might have their wombs removed – a hysterectomy – to help calm them down.

Perhaps that's what convicted child rapist Roman Polanski was hoping for when he dubbed the #MeToo movement 'hysterical'.

The terrible effect on female physiology of studying anything at all – especially science – meant that women were not allowed to train as medical doctors in the UK until the late 19th century. In 1911 there were fewer than 500 women doctors in England and Wales.

In 2018, 45 per cent of registered medical doctors are women, and women outnumber men in British medical schools. There's nothing hard-wired about this change. Our brains aren't made differently now to how they were made a hundred years ago. Rather, they are programmed differently. When prejudice and bad science are no longer in the way, women always prove themselves as capable as men.

I don't believe we are born with gendered brains. The flush of in-utero testosterone that destines some foetuses to be male and others to be female isn't responsible for the way we organise society. Testosterone is the current must-have hormone of choice for the #MenAreKing style of bad science (and I mean 'bad science' in the way that climate-change deniers do bad science). Men need to be paid more. Men shouldn't change nappies. Men need to mate often etc.

There is still a sex war going on – but we have to remember something simple and obvious:

Discrimination of any kind is never, ever rational – it just pretends to be.*

———————

Women fought for education because it is hard to be equal if you are not educated.

In 1869 the Edinburgh Seven were the first women to enrol at any British university, though they weren't allowed to graduate.

———————

* If you want to read more about hormonal effects on brain development, have a look at Cordelia Fine's *Delusions of Gender* and the magnificent *Testosterone Rex*.

The University of London awarded degrees to its first four women students in 1880.

Oxford University didn't allow women to take degrees until 1920.

At Cambridge, although women had their own colleges — Girton and Newnham being the first — women had to wait until 1948 to be awarded full degrees, regardless of how well they did in their exams. Prior to 1948, female graduates were awarded a degree in title only — a titular degree, known, inevitably, as a BA TIT (thanks, guys).

Cambridge continued to set the ratio of female to male undergraduates at 1 in 10 — just let that soak in a second — until 1987. Yes, you did read that correctly — 1987. In practice the ratio was ignored, but I think it is significant that it took so long to remove.

But wherever they were educated, until the mid-'70s, women made up just 23 per cent of the university population of the UK. When I first read this statistic I went straight to the dusty loo next to my scullery at home to look at my matriculation photo. I went to St Catherine's College, Oxford, in 1978, a newish and mixed college. I did a head count of my photo. Of the 166 faces in the photo, 105 were male. So, at around 35 per cent female, St Catz was doing well for its time.

But the thing is, I didn't notice the ratio at the time and I never thought about it afterwards.

And that's how it is with patriarchy – we don't notice the all-male panels, the movies where women are just the love interest, the number of male presenters on TV and radio, the fact that the House of Commons has 208 female MPs, which is great, but nowhere near the 300+ we need for parity – and we do need parity, because women are one half of the population.

I feel sorry for men who have to keep hearing this stuff, because they don't notice it either. They aren't behaving like sexist shits (mainly), it's really, truly and honestly that men in public life is just the norm. We're not gender-blind – in fact, I think we see double – we notice a few women here and there, and we think, oh, this is equality – look, there's a woman. People even say things like, 'Well, the Queen's a woman.' Well, yes, she is, and there won't be another Queen who's a King for a very long time.

Women of my generation were the lucky ones, though. We could go to university, get a degree, and when we came out the other side, we didn't face the Marriage Bar.

The Marriage Bar? This is not a piece of chocolate that made women want to give up work and have babies. The Marriage Bar was all the careers and jobs not open to married women, or the careers and jobs women were obliged to resign from when they got married, so that they could focus on their husband and children. It was legal to sack a woman if she were to get pregnant.

The Marriage Bar remained in place until after the Second World War, but even when it was formally removed, it remained the custom and practice. Employers could refuse to hire women who were married, and fire them perfectly legally if they tried to do what their husbands were doing – have a family and a career.

Graffiti on a loo wall in Camden Town: *Behind every great woman is a man who tried to stop her.*

It wasn't until 1975 that the Sex Discrimination Act made it illegal to manipulate the labour market in favour of men and against women. At last, sex differences – biology – were being uncoupled from gender bias – *you can't do whatever it is you want to do because you're a woman.* So when someone has a moan about women-only selection lists, or positive discrimination to get women moving up the work ladder, remember that we have had only a brief forty years of an attempt at a level playing field for women. We deserve a redress against generational imbalance.

But even now, in 2018, when we've seen how far and how fast women can go when discrimination gets out of the way, people, in all seriousness, come out with nutcase comments like, 'Ah well, where was the female Shakespeare? There was no female Einstein, you know . . .'

The female Einstein was suffering from anorexia scholastica and worrying about what effect equations would have on her womb.

The female Shakespeare, unlike her brother, Will, would have found no work as an actor because women weren't allowed on the London stage back then. She would not have been to grammar school, unlike her brother – and neither Shakespeare's wife nor his daughters could read or write – and how would she have made the three-day journey from

Stratford-upon-Avon to London, with no money of her own?*

Women and money — that's a touchy subject. Women couldn't apply for credit, loans or mortgages in their own right in the UK until 1975. 1975! That was when the Sex Discrimination Act forced banks to treat women as they treated men. Imagine having to ask your father, brother, or husband to guarantee your loan. And how do you own a house when you can't get a mortgage? Women's poverty is linked to our lack of creditworthiness. In many parts of the world, it is still nearly impossible for women to get finance without a male in the mix.

In the UK, the banks fought back against equal credit, arguing that women often gave

---

* Read Virginia Woolf's *A Room of One's Own* for more on women, education, money and creativity.

up work on marriage, or worked part-time and that they didn't earn enough to justify credit – even though five years earlier, in 1970, the Labour Government had introduced the Equal Pay Act. It was the women at the Ford car plant at Dagenham who went on strike in 1968, bringing the British car industry to a standstill, who forced the Government to recognise equal pay for equal work.

Campaigning women.

Noisy women.

Militant women.

Good behaviour didn't get us bank loans or pay rises.

More than fifty years later we're in an almighty row about women's pay. Over 3,000 UK firms who reported in 2018 showed an average gender pay gap of over 18 per cent.[1]

Women doctors – in the majority now, remember – are paid less than men. A BBC investigation in 2018 revealed an average gender pay gap among medical consultants of £14,000.[2] Of the top-earning one hundred consultants, only five are women. In the NHS, six and a half times as many men get the top bonus payments.

Part of the justification for this has been that men are prepared to work longer hours. Well, someone at home is doing the shopping and the cooking and looking after the children, then.

The culture of long hours that kicked off in the 1980s makes it pretty impossible for a working person to have a home-life unless someone other than the working person is making that home-life.

Women go part-time, not because they can't manage the stress or the pressure of work, but because children need time, elderly relatives need time, our friends, the people we love need time, love itself needs time.

And when it comes to being 'prepared' to work long hours, we all know that the true length of a working week for a woman with a family is 24/7.

―――――――

What about promotion? What about the lucrative top jobs and seats on the board?

In companies listed on the Financial Times Stock Exchange 350 Index, only 29 per cent of seats on boards go to women. And in May 2018 a report was published that revealed some of the pitiful excuses why men don't choose women for positions at board level:

All the best women have been snapped up.

We already have a woman on the board so we are done.

There aren't that many women with the right credentials and depth of experience to sit on this board — the issues covered are extremely complex.[3]

(Eek — she'll get anorexia scholastica.)

Is it really because woman don't have the experience business needs?

Perhaps it's that women who do have the experience are likely to be in their fifties – peak years for alpha males, but the decade when women suddenly find that their husband is leaving them for a younger version, that men aren't interested in them sexually any more, that they are, as Ben Broadbent, Deputy Governor of the Bank of England, described the British economy, menopausal.[4] He then dug himself in deeper by saying he just meant past its peak.

There was a dark lesson there – a clue to the way that men think about women. At the moment when a woman is at the top of her game, do her male colleagues see a woman who is past her peak?

Perhaps, in any case, it's not that women don't have the experience, or the skills – perhaps it's that business-think is just too narrow. We don't need women directing policy – whether it's at corporate or government level – like replica men. We need women to bring so much that men aren't bringing.

I am not talking biological essentialism here – I am talking about the way women and girls are raised, because, like it or not, boys and girls are raised differently:

Women are brought up to listen.

Women learn how to be caring.

Women are multi-taskers.

Women are diplomats – skilled at the art of the compromise.

Women look for a solution instead of a stand-off.

Women do the invisible mending that holds a family together.

These are learned skills – not innate skills – but they are skills that companies need at management level. Skills we need in the board-room. And on the world stage.

An alpha male I know – and quite like – defended his rubbish record for promoting women by telling me that with women it's always personal. We take things personally – like not being promoted, I suppose – and we find it harder to make what he called objective decisions.

What is an objective decision?

The world is made of human beings dealing with other human beings.

Every decision that we make – great or small – affects ourselves and others, sometimes count-less others. And it would be better to recognise that we need decision-makers and leaders who can see the human picture, not just the bottom line. The big picture is the human picture.

Ordinary families.

People's lives.

The lives that women see close up and personal.

Life is not a spreadsheet.

And equality is not only about women advancing into territory traditionally held by men. Women have much to teach men, much to offer the world of work.

In my view, a bit more co-operation and a bit less competition would be a management style that benefits men, women and the planet.

More women in charge might have questioned the grotesque pay packets, the dick-swinging risk-taking of the kind that leveraged all our resources and crashed the economy in 2008. The empty pension funds, the savage number-crunching of the gig economy. The two or three jobs a household needs to make ends meet, the increase in children who are neglected, children going hungry, the bleak prospects for so many young people.

When I look at the UK – this rich, reckless country – I feel like Marx and Engels wandering round the blackened, deafening streets of Manchester, wondering why the human race can't do better for its people?

And yes, it's personal.

And I think to myself – well, women have

caught up so far and so fast in a hundred years, so let's make sure women get those seats in parliament — those seats on the board — and let's see if we can't come up with something more creative than Winner Takes All. Winner Takes All is a lousy way to live. It's Stone Age politics with Donald Trump for President.

———

The President of the United States may go down in history as a super-sized reason why the fight for women's equality is everywhere in the news again.

The President believes that powerful men can do what they want to women. Just grab them by the pussy. Movie mogul Harvey Weinstein put that into practice for decades, until brave women called time on the casting couch.

The #MeToo movement, founded by black activist Tarana Burke to tackle sexual violence suffered by young black women, became the hashtag for a global movement against sexual harassment.

The #MeToo movement isn't a return to Victorian values.

Women aren't shrinking violets asking to be protected.

This is about respect.

• That men respect women at work –
  allowing women to get on with their job,
  without leers or jeers.
• That men respect women politically as
  equals.
• That men respect women in the home,
  because one in four women in the world
  has been a victim of domestic violence.
• That men respect women's bodies as not
  for the taking.
• That men stop using pornography as a
  way of distorting and disrespecting
  women's sexuality.

- That men do not use social media as sex-war hate mail.
- That men stop raping women.

Don't protect me – respect me.

When women are respected we don't need protection.

And it's not just the #MeToo movement.

Laura Bates' website Everyday Sexism does what it says on the tin. This website is a daily resource for women who are learning to stop thinking that casual or direct abuse is normal. Hate-Male wherever found needs to be called out.

Time's Up – the pressure group for equality in the workplace – has the vocal support of the Duchess of Sussex, Meghan Markle.

Action Aid's My Body Is Mine is championed by Emma Thompson. Recently she spoke to Jenni Murray on *Woman's Hour*, pointing out that the fight against sexual harassment is generational – in her mother's day it was, 'he's just being nice, or he's taking an interest in you'. For her generation, unwanted sexual attention was part of a price to be paid for freedom and success. For her daughter's generation, though, she believes things are changing.

This reasonable and optimistic view (the polar opposite of 'hysterical') is borne out by the remarkable Emma Watson's donation of a million pounds to the new UK Justice and Equality Fund.

Such initiatives are not the hobbies of fancy women flashing their privilege. These are women *using* their privilege, their platform, their power to support women all over the world who want something very simple – an end to sexism.

And what's wrong with that?

Of course, women will fight amongst themselves about the kinds of problems they face, the scale of the problems, and the solutions. How can it be otherwise? Political groups never agree. One hundred years ago Millicent Fawcett advocated law-abiding lobbying to get the vote. The Pankhursts preferred to get down and dirty.

Men disagree amongst themselves but they have learned to make common cause when it matters. Women are learning to do the same.

In any case, if we're going to end sexism, men and women alike will have to work together.

There is no other way.

And there is no better way.

I don't want a world where men and women can't flirt with each other, can't take pleasure in beauty, can't enjoy sex or sexual power or sexual difference, but biology is not destiny – and there is no reason why women should not be equal, why women should not be safe at home or at work, just because they are women.

And as our coming revolution is one where we prepare to share the planet with self-created non-human intelligence – biology as destiny seems very old-fashioned indeed.

———————

Let's have a look at the future.

The change coming is bigger than the industrial revolution. More far-reaching than any tech innovation we have seen so far.

Alan Turing's code-breaking pal from Bletchley Park, Jack Good, called it The Last Invention.

Jack Good was Stanley Kubrick's adviser on the film *2001: A Space Odyssey*, famous for its creepy computer HAL.

For Jack Good, the last invention will be Artificial Intelligence. After that, he believed, the major decisions won't be ours to make.

Good made that prophecy in 1965 – here we are today, and it is starting to happen.

We already shout at Alexa in the kitchen and Siri on our smartphone – algorithms suggest to us what we might like to buy next. Many people spend more time communing with their devices than they do with humans. We're changing the nature of human interaction.

In Shanghai, there is a branch of the China Construction Bank which is human-free. Robots deal with your request. Robot security guards patrol Chinese railway stations. Robot waiters are doing their best to serve noodles prepared by robot chefs.

In Hong Kong, Hanson Laboratories have launched a glamorous robot called Sophia, touted as the future of AI. Sophia was recently granted full citizenship of Saudi Arabia – meaning she has more rights than Saudi women.

Actually, I am half in love with Sophia. She is clearly a democrat, and doesn't think we need to live in a gender-bound world of binaries: (He/She/Female/Male). If you haven't seen her in action, have a look at her on YouTube.

Robots are tools and could revolutionise the

world of work, so that we don't have to do boring repetitive jobs that we hate. It's a great idea, but human beings who are put out of work will need to be re-trained or re-skilled. Or be given a basic income. There are a lot of questions that will affect us all, male and female, but for me, the big question is: Where are the women in the brave new world that is being designed for us right now?

The problem is that women aren't going into computer science – about 18 per cent of computer science graduates are women.

We know from our experience of the last hundred years that this has nothing to do with women's hard-wired aptitude for maths or engineering. There is no disease called anorexia silicona whereby women's reproductive systems will blow up if they spend all day working on software.

We do know that the geeky frat-dorm, asocial, small-screen world of much that is techie is unappealing to a lot of women.

Melinda Gates has said that Silicon Valley needs to fix its gender problem; it is hostile and sexist.[5]

In the USA, Project Include is an initiative whose goal is to encourage women into the tech industry. Project Include notes that women in tech are evaluated on their appearance and personality, while men pride themselves on looking dress-disinterested because scruffy hoodie signals distracted genius if you are male – not if you are female.

That old mystic shibboleth, genius, has reared its head again. You need to be gifted to do computer science. And although, yeah, women can learn to be doctors and lawyers, maths teachers, basic programmers – like the top end of art, music, literature, painting, women's brains just don't seem to cut it for the big-bucks breakthroughs.

Women trying to launch tech start-ups are advised by Project Include to get a male on board – even if he doesn't know anything. It reassures investors, who see the tech future as a male future.

At present, females in tech are there all right. As sexbots. All three holes are the same size, and fully penetrable. Breasts are large, waists small, and hair can be changed. Sexbots aren't like blow-up dolls; sexbots will talk to you. Some come with family mode so that they can entertain the children with fairy stories and jokes.

Sexbots are cheaper than prostitutes – once you have made the initial outlay – and they are a lot less trouble than real women. Men don't have to pretend to be interested in their opinions or buy them dinner.

Go online and look at some at the comments men make about sexbots:

At last a women who does what I tell her.

She doesn't talk in bed.

This serves feminists right.

No running costs.

Remember that 1975 movie *The Stepford Wives*?

Where the guys replace their bolshie women with submissive replicas . . .?

In China, a culture that values males over females, the decades-long one-child policy has left a dramatic male-to-female shortfall. There are 33 million more Chinese men than women. China has a booming sexbot industry. For anyone interested, just google it and see for yourself the racks of torsos swinging along the conveyor belt to have their heads screwed on, the extra-long legs, the choice of wig, the 'creators' talking about the social service they are offering all those lonely men.

Robot concubines have a serious future.

AI could be the best thing that has happened to humankind – or the worst thing that has happened to women ever.* In the UK, networkers and organisers Women Leading in

---

* Ada Lovelace (1815–52) was the daughter of Lord Byron and the first person to imagine a software program for Babbage's analytical engine – the world's first concept-computer.

AI are encouraging women to join the debate about our future, and to become part of policy-making. The Ada Lovelace Institute, founded in 2018, will seek to put diversity and equality at the core of the coming AI revolution.

Women have had just a hundred years to become players in every bit of the present day. It is essential that we don't allow the future to become a new exclusion zone.

———————

This year Suffragist Millicent Fawcett joins eleven all-male statues in Parliament Square. Millicent was the President of the National Union of Women's Suffrage Societies.

Her sister – just so you know – was Elizabeth Garrett Anderson, the first female doctor in the UK.

We honour great men.

We should honour great women.

The statue is there because one of our

modern heroines, Caroline Criado Perez, campaigned to get it there. Criado Perez is the woman who persuaded the Bank of England Governor, Mark Carney, to keep a woman's face – other than the Queen's – on a British banknote. So we got the Jane Austen tenner.

Thanks to Caroline Criado Perez, British sculptor Gillian Wearing was commissioned to make the statue. Millicent Fawcett holds out a banner that says COURAGE CALLS TO COURAGE EVERYWHERE.

I am a fiction writer, so I know that the stories we hear and the stories we tell have a huge influence on us. Society changes as we tell different stories – when we tell the story again.

Women in the 20th century kickstarted a more inclusive history – a better set of stories.

History – His-story – had to include Her-story.

Women in the 21st century – young women,

a new generation of women – are speaking out louder and stronger. For social and sexual equality. For an end to the policing of women by religion. For the value of women to be recognised. For our contribution to be rewarded. For the freedom to walk by day and by night without fear. To know that our bodies are ours. Never to be shamed for being a woman. To love without coercion. To feel desire. To bear and raise children in peace and with resources. To be an equal part of the future as it happens.

Women are not an after-thought.

Women are not inferior.

Women belong in the world.

———

Speak it. Write it. Read it. Make it visible. Let it be heard.

Let courage call to courage everywhere.

Freedom or Death

Introduction to *Freedom or Death*

Look at the title of this speech. It's brave, it's uncompromising, it's a rallying cry for women then and now. But – and this is a big but – why is the penalty of freedom, for women, violence on a scale that too often ends in death?

A woman walks through the city at night – she risks rape, a beating, maybe murder.

A woman rows with her male partner at home – one in four women are victims of domestic violence.

Across the world, women can't get legal

abortion – so women risk maiming, infection or death in backstreet clinics.

A young girl, Malala Yousafzai, spoke up for education for women in Pakistan – she was shot in the head.

Forced marriages – almost 750 million women and girls alive today were married before their eighteenth birthday. There are no statistics for women over the age of eighteen in forced marriages.

Genital mutilation – at least 200 million women and girls alive today have been cut, routinely before the age of five.

Trafficking – women and girls represent 71 per cent of global trafficking victims.

Domestic violence – 50 per cent of women murdered globally are murdered by their partners or by family members. For men, that figure is less than 6 per cent.

Not all men are violent, but all men need to work with women to combat the routine and extreme violence directed against women all over the world.*

Jeanette Winterson, September 2018

---

* All statistics in this introduction are from UN Women

Freedom or Death
by Emmeline Pankhurst

Delivered in Hartford, Connecticut,
on 13 November 1913

I do not come here as an advocate, because whatever position the suffrage movement may occupy in the United States of America, in England it has passed beyond the realm of advocacy and it has entered into the sphere of practical politics. It has become the subject of revolution and civil war, and so tonight I am not here to advocate woman suffrage. American suffragists can do that very well for themselves.

I am here as a soldier who has temporarily left the field of battle in order to explain – it seems strange it should have to be explained – what civil war is like when civil war is waged by women. I am not only here as a soldier temporarily absent from the field at battle; I am here – and that, I think, is the strangest part of my coming – I am here as a person who, according to the law courts of my country, it has been decided, is of no value to the community at all; and I am adjudged because of my life to be a dangerous person, under sentence of penal servitude in a convict prison.

It is not at all difficult if revolutionaries come to you from Russia, if they come to you from China, or from any other part of the world, if they are men. But since I am a woman it is necessary to explain why women have adopted revolutionary methods in order to win the rights of citizenship. We women, in trying to make our case clear, always have to make as part of our argument, and urge upon men in

56

our audience the fact – a very simple fact – that women are human beings.

Suppose the men of Hartford had a grievance, and they laid that grievance before their legislature, and the legislature obstinately refused to listen to them, or to remove their grievance, what would be the proper and the constitutional and the practical way of getting their grievance removed? Well, it is perfectly obvious at the next general election the men of Hartford would turn out that legislature and elect a new one.

But let the men of Hartford imagine that they were not in the position of being voters at all, that they were governed without their consent being obtained, that the legislature turned an absolutely deaf ear to their demands, what would the men of Hartford do then? They couldn't vote the legislature out. They would have to choose; they would have to make a choice of two evils: they would either have to submit indefinitely to an unjust state of affairs, or they would have to rise up and adopt some of the antiquated means by which men in the past got their grievances remedied.

Your forefathers decided that they must have representation for taxation, many, many years ago. When they felt they couldn't wait any longer, when they laid all the arguments before an obstinate British government that they could think of, and when their arguments were absolutely disregarded, when every other means had failed, they began by the tea party at Boston, and they went on until they had won the independence of the United States of America.

It is about eight years since the word militant was first used to describe what we were doing. It was not militant at all, except that it provoked militancy on the part of those who were opposed to it. When women asked questions in political meetings and failed to get answers, they were not doing anything militant.

In Great Britain it is a custom, a time-honoured one, to ask questions of candidates for parliament and ask questions of members of the government. No man was ever put out of a public meeting for asking a question. The first people who were put out of a political meeting for asking questions, were women; they were brutally ill-used; they found themselves in jail before 24 hours had expired.

We were called militant, and we were quite willing to accept the name. We were determined to press this question of the enfranchisement of women to the point where we were no longer to be ignored by the politicians.

You have two babies very hungry and wanting to be fed. One baby is a patient baby, and waits indefinitely until its mother is ready to feed it. The other baby is an impatient baby and cries lustily, screams and kicks and makes everybody unpleasant until it is fed. Well, we know perfectly well which baby is attended to first. That is the whole history of politics. You have to make more noise than anybody else, you have to make yourself more obtrusive than anybody else, you have to fill all the papers more than anybody else, in fact you have to be there all the time and see that they do not snow you under.

When you have warfare things happen; people suffer; the noncombatants suffer as well as the combatants. And so it happens in civil war. When your forefathers threw the tea into Boston Harbour, a good many women had to go without their tea. It has always seemed to me an extraordinary thing that you did not follow it up by throwing the whiskey overboard; you sacrificed the women; and there is a good deal of warfare for which men take a great deal of glorification which has involved more practical sacrifice on women than it has on any man. It always has been so. The grievances of those who have got power, the influence of those who have got power commands a great deal of attention; but the wrongs and the grievances of those people who have no power at all are apt to be absolutely ignored. That is the history of humanity right from the beginning.

Well, in our civil war people have suffered, but you cannot make omelettes without breaking eggs; you cannot have civil war without damage to something. The great thing is to see that no more damage is done than is absolutely necessary, that you do just as much as will arouse enough feeling to bring about peace, to bring about an honourable peace for the combatants; and that is what we have been doing.

We entirely prevented stockbrokers in London from telegraphing to stockbrokers in Glasgow and vice versa: for one whole day telegraphic communication was entirely stopped. I am not going to tell you how it was done. I am not going to tell you how the women got to the mains and cut the wires; but it was done. It was done, and it was proved to the authorities that weak women, suffrage women, as we are supposed to be, had enough ingenuity to create a situation of that kind. Now, I ask you, if women can do that, is there any limit to what we can do except the limit we put upon ourselves?

If you are dealing with an industrial revolution, if you get the men and women of one class rising up against the men and women of another class, you can locate the difficulty; if there is a great industrial strike, you know exactly where the violence is and how the warfare is going to be waged; but in our war against the government you can't locate it. We wear no mark; we belong to every class; we permeate every class of the community from the highest to the lowest; and so you see in the woman's civil war the dear men of my country are discovering it is absolutely impossible to deal with it: you cannot locate it, and you cannot stop it.

'Put them in prison,' they said, 'that will

stop it.' But it didn't stop it at all: instead of the women giving it up, more women did it, and more and more and more women did it until there were 300 women at a time, who had not broken a single law, only 'made a nuisance of themselves' as the politicians say.

Then they began to legislate. The British government has passed more stringent laws to deal with this agitation than it ever found necessary during all the history of political agitation in my country. They were able to deal with the revolutionaries of the Chartists' time; they were able to deal with the trades union agitation; they were able to deal with the revolutionaries later on when the Reform Acts were passed: but the ordinary law has not sufficed to curb insurgent women. They had to dip back into the Middle Ages to find a means of repressing the women in revolt.

They have said to us, government rests upon force, the women haven't force, so they must submit. Well, we are showing them that government does not rest upon force at all: it rests upon consent. As long as women consent to be unjustly governed, they can be, but directly women say, 'We withhold our consent, we will not be governed any longer so long as that government is unjust.' Not by the forces of civil war can you govern the very weakest woman. You can kill that woman, but she escapes you then; you cannot govern her. No power on earth can govern a human being, however feeble, who withholds his or her consent.

When they put us in prison at first, simply for taking petitions, we submitted; we allowed them to dress us in prison clothes; we allowed them to put us in solitary confinement; we allowed them to put us amongst the most degraded of criminals; we learned of some of the appalling evils of our so-called civilisation that we could not have learned in any other way. It was valuable experience, and we were glad to get it.

I have seen men smile when they heard the words 'hunger strike', and yet I think there are very few men today who would be prepared to adopt a 'hunger strike' for any cause. It is only people who feel an intolerable sense of oppression who would adopt a means of that kind. It means you refuse food until you are at death's door, and then the authorities have to choose between letting you die, and letting you go; and then they let the women go.

Now, that went on so long that the government felt that they were unable to cope. It was [then] that, to the shame of the British government, they set the example to authorities all over the world of feeding sane, resisting human beings by force. There may be doctors in this meeting: if so, they know it is one thing to feed by force an insane person; but it is quite another thing to feed a sane, resisting human being who resists with every nerve and with every fibre of her body the indignity and the outrage of forcible feeding. Now, that was done in England, and the government thought they had crushed us. But they found that it did not quell the agitation, that more and more women came in and even passed that terrible ordeal, and they were obliged to let them go.

Then came the legislation – the 'Cat and Mouse Act'. The home secretary said: 'Give me the power to let these women go when they are at death's door, and leave them at liberty under license until they have recovered their health again and then bring them back.' It was passed to repress the agitation, to make the women yield – because that is what it has really come to, ladies and gentlemen. It has come to a battle between the women and the government as to who shall yield first, whether they will yield and give us the vote, or whether we will give up our agitation.

Well, they little know what women are. Women are very slow to rouse, but once they are aroused, once they are determined, nothing on earth and nothing in heaven will make women give way; it is impossible. And so this 'Cat and Mouse Act' which is being used against women today has failed. There are women lying at death's door, recovering enough strength to undergo operations, who have not given in and won't give in, and who will be prepared, as soon as they get up from their sick beds, to go on as before. There are women who are being carried from their sick beds on stretchers into meetings. They are too weak to speak, but they go amongst their fellow workers just to show that their spirits are unquenched, and that their spirit is alive, and they mean to go on as long as life lasts.

Now, I want to say to you who think women cannot succeed, we have brought the government of England to this position, that it has to face this alternative: either women are to be killed or women are to have the vote. I ask American men in this meeting, what would you say if in your state you were faced with that alternative, that you must either kill them or give them their citizenship? Well, there is only one answer to that alternative, there is only one way out – you must give those women the vote.

You won your freedom in America when you had the revolution, by bloodshed, by sacrificing human life. You won the civil war by the sacrifice of human life when you decided to emancipate the negro. You have left it to women in your land, the men of all civilised countries have left it to women, to work out their own salvation. That is the way in which we women of England are doing. Human life for us is sacred, but we say if any life is to be sacrificed it shall be ours; we won't do it ourselves, but we will put the enemy in the position where they will have to choose between giving us freedom or giving us death.

So here am I. I come in the intervals of prison appearance. I come after having been four times imprisoned under the 'Cat and Mouse Act', probably going back to be re-arrested as soon as I set my foot on British soil. I come to ask you to help to win this fight. If we win it, this hardest of all fights, then, to be sure, in the future it is going to be made easier for women all over the world to win their fight when their time comes.

Endnotes

1 Alexandra Topping, Caelainn Barr and Pamela Duncan, 'Gender pay gap figures reveal eight in 10 UK firms pay men more', *Guardian*, 4 April 2018, accessed 29 August 2018.
2 Nick Triggle, 'Top women doctors lose out in NHS pay stakes', BBC News, 16 February 2018, accessed 29 August 2018.
3 Department for Business, Energy and Industrial Strategy, 'Revealed: The worst explanations for not appointing women to FTSE company boards', www.gov.uk, 31 May 2018, accessed 29 August 2018.

4 Anna Isaac, 'Bank of England deputy warns UK economy entering "menopausal phase"', *Telegraph*, 16 May 2018, accessed 29 August 2018.

5 Melinda Gates, interview by Gillian B. White, *The Atlantic*, 16 March 2017, accessed 29 August 2018.

JEANETTE WINTERSON was born
in Manchester and read English at Oxford,
during which time she wrote her first novel,
the Whitbread Award-winning *Oranges
Are Not the Only Fruit*. Since then she has
published many other novels – including
The Passion, *Sexing the Cherry*, *Written on
the Body*, *The PowerBook* and *The Daylight
Gate* – a collection of short stories, a book
of essays, books for children and a memoir,
*Why Be Happy When You Could Be
Normal?*. She has adapted her work for TV,
film and stage, was awarded an OBE in 2006
and a CBE in 2018 for services to literature.
Her books are published in 32 countries.

@Wintersonworld | jeanettewinterson.com